TOTALLY TERRIFIC TEAM THEMES

Written and created by
Christie Northrup
The Lemon Aid Lady

Cover design by
Steve James

Published by
CANet Publishing   Dallas, TX 75065

PUBLISHED BY
CANet Publishing

Totally Terrific Team Themes, Copyright 1999 by Christie Northrup. All rights reserved. Permission is granted for the owner of this book to reproduce the invitations in the Totally Terrific Team Treasure section of this book for personal, non-commercial use. Other than these invitations, no portion of this book may be reproduced, stored in a retrieval system, or transmitted in any form or by any means—electronic, mechanical, photocopy, recording, or any other—except for brief quotations in printed reviews with source reference, without the prior written permission of the author.

Printed in the United States of America

Dedicated to
The hundreds of women
(and some men)
with whom I had the great
privilege to recruit, teach,
and work with.

Our team meetings were
Totally Terrific...
thanks to each of you!

How to Use this Book

Objective The objective of these two pages is to explain how to use this Totally Terrific Team Theme book and adapt it to the needs of your individual team.

While each Team Theme has fun and entertaining ideas, there must be a reason for holding the meeting. The objective is this reason as well as the outcome you want to achieve after you and the members have left the meeting.

Invitation
Hand Out Most important events *invite,* rather than simply notify, the guest. A written invitation positions this as a special event, not just something that the person is expected to show up to. Invitations for each of the 18 Team Themes are provided at the end of the book.

As owner of the book, you have permission to photocopy the invitations *for your own personal use for your team.* Suggestion: Make a copy of the invitation, then fill in the blanks with your information and make the rest of the copies from this second copy. This way, you can reuse the invitations for future meetings.

In addition to sending an invitation, attaching an additional visual reminder helps to entice the team member to attend. These ideas are listed in this section of each Team Theme as "Hand Out."

Bring Along Involving members even before they arrive at the meeting increases attendance. Each Team Theme lists something for the members to bring along. If you use the "Bring Along" idea, write this on the invitation if it is not already printed. People are usually curious as to why they are bringing what you are requesting and many times this curiosity is the motivation for attending.

Setting for Success As people enter the meeting room, have props and other items on display so the feeling of the Team Theme begins when they walk in the door.

How to Use this Book

Team Theme Talk This is the "meat" of the meeting; the lesson to be taught. Adapt to your team's needs.

Note: All Team Themes contain a lot of information. You do not have to use everything at one meeting. Choose the appropriate parts for your situation.

Activity To reinforce what you taught in the Team Theme Talk, have members participate in the activity.

Applause Awards Recognition is a major part of a productive meeting. People like to be shown appreciation for their efforts. While honoring those who have excelled in personal performance is important, some members will never meet that criteria. However, each team member's contribution is important. Therefore, the Applause Awards do a *TWIST* on the traditional reward ideas. These Awards coincide with the theme of the meeting. The idea is to catch people doing something right and honor them in front of their peers.

Challenge "The Proof of the Presentation is in Personal Performance." This is the ending thought at Lemon Aid Seminars. People can get excited and motivated at a meeting, but what really matters are the actions after. The challenge gives specific ideas of how to take what is taught and turn it into activity and results.

Food for Thought If you choose to serve food at the meeting, have the refreshments connect to the theme for an additional reminder of the ideas you taught.

Picture Yourself A Winner

Objective *For team members to learn how to mentally imagine and visualize their future goals, and then plan the necessary steps to create the picture of success they want to see and experience.*

Invitation
Hand out

Frame the written invitation inside of inexpensive picture frames purchased at a dollar store or found at garage sales. Or, write the information on adding machine tape, roll up, and put inside the black, plastic canisters film comes in. On the outside of the canister, attach a label that says, "You're invited to Picture Yourself a Winner."

Bring Along

Each member is encouraged to bring a picture of themselves doing something they love to do or have achieved. Examples are vacations, employment promotions, achievement recognitions, high school or college yearbook photos (photocopy is fine), or even a childhood event.

Setting for Success

Have camera, film, photos, photo albums, etc. on display.

Team Theme Talk

Pictures are important because they remind us of times past and evoke mental and emotional memories when we view them. You can predict the future of your accomplishments by "Picturing Yourself a Winner" before the event happens. How? First, by physically taking a picture and associating yourself with the goal. If your goal is to take a trip to England, get pictures of things that remind you of England such as palaces, green country sides, Big Ben, etc. (you can get these from local travel agents). Then, paste a picture of yourself next to these English reminders. Display the pictures where you'll see them often.

The next step is to have the right equipment. A camera with the right kind of film and necessary attachments (telephoto lens, etc.) is a must to take pictures. This means you need the proper equipment to physically and mentally see yourself achieving your goal. This tool is a **written list of the steps** you must take to develop the goal into reality. Look at this list every day and plan your activities accordingly. This visualization puts your goal into clear focus. Otherwise, your goals are fuzzy; your eyes will hurt when you look at your goal, so you'll take your focus off of it and never see the picture of success.

Picture Yourself A Winner

After taking pictures, the roll of film must be developed. You must enjoy the results of your goal and reload the camera. This is done by putting the pictures of your goal achievement in a photo album where you can remind yourself of your success and share your memories with others. Then, create another future goal so you can continue to "Picture Yourself a Winner!"

Activity

Have items such as construction paper, glue sticks, magazines, company brochures, etc. available so members can create a "Future Photo." Use the picture they brought of themselves along with photos already taken of the team etc., to represent these future goals.

Or, have each person write their goal in big, bold type on a poster board. Then take pictures of them holding their goal signs. Get double prints developed. You keep one and send the other to the individual. If you have a tangible object that is their goal (furniture, car, etc.) take the picture of them next to this object.

Applause Awards

Camera Bug - Have team members open their wallets. Who has the most pictures of their families?
Capture Someone doing Something Right - Your choice of some outstanding accomplishment since the last meeting.
Preserve the Praise - For the person who is always complimenting others on the team; sort of the cheerleader.

Challenge

Pictures are worth thousands of words. However, a goal needs to be in clear focus. So, in addition to the goal they have "pictured" themselves meeting in the Activity Section, encourage them to make a step-by-step plan of how they'll meet this goal. Suggest they read this goal and plan three to five times a day. When a photographic image is embedded in their minds, the goal really will develop into a beautiful picture.

Food for Thought

To keep in the camera theme, serve something the color of most cameras: black and white. Oreo Cookies and milk are an easy idea.

Office Essentials

Objective — Even with all the high-tech equipment we have in our offices, some basic items will always be necessary to run a efficient business. Along the same lines, while we learn many innovative ideas for building businesses, the basics remain constant.

Invitations
Hand out — Fax the invitation to those with fax machines, or send via snail mail with a small office item attached (staple, paper clip, post note, etc.).

Bring Along — Request that everyone bring a rubber band. Have extras on hand at the meeting for those who forget.

Setting for Success — Create a display of office items such as adding machines, phones, file folders, staplers, etc.

Team Theme Talk — This Team Theme Talk will show the correlation between common, simple, office items and mastering essential business skills. Have items such as scissors, tape, glue, pen, eraser, paper punch, paper clip, etc. on display.
Selling Skills: Sometimes we get caught up in all the fancy, new-fangled features of our product and forget the customer usually needs a basic explanation of the product's features tied to the benefits for them. After they have this knowledge, and are ready to know more, additional features can be explained. Here is a good exercise to teach features versus benefits and to create a simple presentation.

Form groups of two people each. One way to create groups to get more ideas flowing (so people don't always work with the same friends all the time) is to create sets with names of office items on small slips of paper. For example, if twenty people are in attendance, write names of ten different items using two slips for each item. Each person chooses a slip, then teams up with the person who has the identical item name.

Now that groups are formed, one person is the customer, and the other is the consultant (or whatever term your company uses for its salespeople). (On the slips of paper you used to form the groups, you could already have assigned this. A slip that says "stamp pad," could have "customer" on one and "consultant" on the other.) Instruct the "consultant" to sell the item to the "customer" just by listing features. This sounds like an easy exercise, but because the item is so basic, features have to really be thought about. Once features are listed, the "customer" tells the "consultant" what she needs and/or consultant can ask questions to discover the customer's needs. Then the consultant must convert the features into the benefits

Office Essentials

that will fill the customer's needs. This exercise also helps to hone listening skills. An example of dialog for this can be found in the **Lemon Aid Deed Alphabet** on page 15. If time allows, reverse the roles with different office items.

Recruiting/Teaching Skills: Have pencils and paper for each person along with a photocopied page from a book or magazine, preferably text that is applicable to the business (such as **The Lemon Aid Books**). Instruct each person to copy the text from the paper onto the paper you gave them. Use about three to five minutes for writing. At the end of the time, ask the group if this is the best way to transfer information from one source to another. Of course, the answer is NO! Ask for a better way (copier, printer, or scanner). Liken this to growing a business. If you have to personally copy all your efforts, your business will barely grow, and you'll lose interest because of the boring, lengthy task. However, when the business opportunity is enthusiastically shared and taught, everyone benefits!

Activity

Using the rubber bands that everyone brought (or you gave), do an object lesson. Dangle the rubber band loosely. Ask, "Is this rubber band fulfilling its purpose?" Of course the answer is no. Then, stretch the band around a bundle of pens. Explain that the rubber band was not useful until it was *stretched*. To fulfill our purposes and goals, we too must stretch.

Applause Awards

Stick to It Award - *For the person who met and overcame a challenge. Give a glue stick, tape, or stapler as an award*
Cut Up Award - *For the person who keeps every laughing and creates fun for the team. Give scissors as an award*
Frequent Filer - *For the person who is known for being organized;*

Challenge

For sales growth, have each team member focus on one product, line, or service to dissect and understand the features and how to translate into benefits for the customer.

For recruiting growth, encourage each person to find just two people to interview. One who is just like they are, one who appears to be opposite. If everyone talked to two prime people, the team will soon double!

Food for Thought

Have an assortment of the kinds of treats people keep at their desks: hard, wrapped candy, gum, pretzels, snack mix.

Become a Best Seller

Objective — *Selling books is a big business; however, only a few make the best-selling list. Team members will learn how becoming a best seller in the company is related to writing, publishing, and marketing a best selling book.*

Invitation
Hand Out — Wrap the invitation in the Team Treasures Section around a small notebook to give the appearance of the invitation being a book, or just mail the invitation as it is.

Setting for Success — Have a mini library of best selling books for team members to look at. Use your own or visit the library. See reading recommendations in the Back to School; Back to Work theme, Chapter 15.

Bring Along — Request each team member to bring along a book. This book can be the one they love the most, the one they are reading right now, the one they have read the most. The reason isn't important, as long as there is some personal meaning to the book they bring.

Team Theme Talk — What creates a best-selling book will also create a best-selling salesperson.

The Title: While you don't need to rename yourself, find something about you that will be memorable to your customers. For example, The Lemon Aid Lady. I write books and teach seminars on business-building topics, but people remember me because I use the lemon as a personal "icon" or title. I also promote my slogan/mission statement which is: "My specialty is teaching you how to *TWIST* Sour Situations into Sweet Successes and Juicy Profits."

The Cover: Even though the saying says we shouldn't judge a book by its cover, we all do--either consciously or subconsciously. Therefore, the appearance of a salesperson is critical in forming a favorable first impression. Expensive, stylish clothes are not as important as cleanliness and good grooming. For more suggestions, refer to **The Lemon Aid Deed Alphabet,** pages 8-10, and 89.

The Content: You've attracted a customer because your "cover" was appealing. As the customer works with you, be sure your content is valuable. Are you knowledgeable about your product/service? Are you interested in the customer? Do you attempt to match her needs with the benefits of your product?

Testimonials: What are other people saying about you? Notice books which list the testimonials of readers. Sometimes people buy books because they are endorsed by a celebrity or a person well-known in the industry. These opinions encourage the purchase of the

Become a Best Seller

the book. Ask your customers for their opinions and their permission to publish them. Create a portfolio from these.

An Editor. A book editor is like a sales leader. She doesn't write the book, but guides the writer to perfect the work. Are you listening to your leader, are you taking suggestions from and giving encouragement to each other?

A Publisher. Most people believe they must sell their manuscript to a publisher before a book can be printed. So, the book sits in a desk drawer until the magical acceptance arrives. Contrary to popular belief, the book doesn't become a best seller because it is published by a large publisher. Many best sellers become such because the author did the publishing and the promoting. As a salesperson, representing a quality product or being part of a top-performing team does not a best seller make. You must go out and tell the world about you and your product. You create your own best selling salesperson!

Activity

As members bring their books, make a display. During Team Talk, use these examples to show the cover, content, etc. Then, have each person tell why he chose to bring his selection. Compare the reasons to ideas for being a best seller. For example, if the book was one "I couldn't put down," brainstorm ways of being a best seller where people won't want you to leave because your content is so good, etc.

Applause Awards

Match recognition to these "best-selling" book titles:
How to Win Customers and Influence Hostesses: For person who held or scheduled the most new demonstrations.
Chicken Soup for the Best Sharing Soul: For everyone who recruited a new person.
Sell and Grow Rich: Person with highest commission check for last week/month or tops in sales.

Challenge

Using the idea of a "Best Seller List", give each team member a blank sheet of paper. Have them decide where on the Best Seller List they want to place in terms of dollars sold/activities held/profits made and then *write their name in that spot.* Next, and most importantly, have them *list the Top Ten activities necessary* to become the Best Seller in that position. The top list doesn't mean they compete against others, more important, against themselves.

Food for Thought

Serve something that resembles the shape of a book, like Fig Bars, or make bar cookies.

Cures for What Ails your Business

Objective
To teach team members that like our physical bodies, sometimes our business gets ill. Recognizing the illness and seeking a cure is the key, rather than ignoring the symptoms and having the illness become terminal--where the business fails or owner gives up. Additionally, working on the business daily creates a healthy business, like eating good food and proper rest maintains our physical body.

Invitation
Hand Out
Write the meeting information on tongue depressors or attach depressors to written invitations. If you use the invitations in Team Treasures, be sure to print on <u>white</u> paper.

Bring Along
Ask each person to bring an item from a First Aid Kit.

Setting for Success
If possible, have room set up like the waiting room in a doctor's office. Each person signs in with a receptionist, have magazines on a table and the D.R. (could be you) is dressed in white coat/scrubs.

Team Theme Talk
A fun way to present these ideas is in skit form. Pre-assign individuals to act out the following diseases along with appropriate props. Have one person be the D.R. (director of recovery) who will reveal the cures. Adapt to your business and situation.

Motivation Measles: Actor walks in with several letter "M's" taped to clothing. Moans about not being motivated. D.R. prescribes a shot of "whyshe"--asking the person "why" she began her business, why she enjoys the work, etc. Once the "whys" are established the *reasons* for moving to action (motivation) should be apparent. D.R takes the M's and turns them upside down to become W's then reminds patient that motivation needs to come from within. Listening to tapes, reviewing written goals, and/or attending sales meetings or seminars could also be prescribed for therapy.

Worry Wart Ulcer: This patient walks in stuttering "Wwwwhat if.....? Every time the D.R. gives a suggestion, she still shakes and stutters the "wwwhat if?" question. D.R. teaches her to ask "Why not?" and to take action by making decisions.

Apathetic Aches. This patient is so apathetic she doesn't even want to go out of her way to visit the D.R. After persuading her to come into the office, the patient whines about not wanting to get involved in attending sales meetings, planning sessions, etc. Then she aches when new ideas are suggested and she wasn't consulted! D.R. gives a prescription to get involved by attending all sales meetings.

Blaming Bacteria: Patient comes in with his index finger pointing at the D.R. and begins blaming. "I'm late because someone took my

Cures for What Ails your Business

parking space, then someone else wouldn't hold the elevator for me." During the conversation with the D.R., the patient continually "points her finger" at others for her trouble. Blaming Bacteria is immediately diagnosed. D.R. uses a splint to put the three fingers pointing back at the patient out in front so the pointer finger is "gone." D.R. reminds patient when we blame others and "point a finger" three are pointing back at her; she must take responsibility for her actions.

Broken Bones: Have patient come limping in to see the D.R. limping and complaining that she can't call anyone because her fingers hurt. Her disease is diagnosed as "broken bones." The only way to heal is to start dialing phone numbers and talking to customers!

Labor Pains: Patient complains that all tasks are too difficult. She doesn't have time or desire to do what is necessary to build her business. This disease is also called laziness. The only antidote is to get out and work the pains away! (Have this person look pregnant!)

Lock Jaw: Patient is at loss of words when talking to customers; doesn't know what to say. D.R. prescribes attending all sales educational events and seminars available and then to open wide!

Activity

Have each person show what item they brought from their First Aid kit. As a team, create a business First Aid kit. Examples: Bandage - put over the little cuts and don't let them fester into big problems. Gauze - Keep the reason you're doing your business in front of you; I'm involved in this business "begauze..." First Aid Cream - Keep in touch with leader and attend sales events to keep covered. Be creative!

Applause Awards

Whooping Coughed up the Sales Award: For the top seller or most improved over the previous month or quarter.

Ideal Patient Award: For the person who has the most patience in building a business. Consistently works and doesn't complain when results are not immediate.

M.D. Award: Stands for "Mighty Determined." To award someone who works and performs against all and any odds.

Challenge

Most of the business illnesses can be cured by taking action. On a prescription form, fill out a "prescription" for all that ails: "Lick the business blues by opening your mouth, getting to know your customer, and following through on sales and service."

Food for Thought

Serve blue popsicles or suckers. Encourage members to lick the blues by opening their mouth and taking action. This will soothe throats and promote activity and results.

Recipe for Success

Objective
Just as combining ingredients together creates delicious dishes and remarkable recipes, working together as team members can create many Sweet Successes and Juicy Profits--individually and as a team!

Invitation Hand Out
Use a recipe as the invitation and attach the result. For example, give a recipe for a cookie and add the cookie along with the recipe. Headline: Learn the Recipe for Success at team meeting...

Bring Along
Use one of your favorite recipes for a cake or cookies (or use the suggested one for Outstanding Oatmeal Team Cake). Divide the ingredients among the team and assign each person to bring one of the items.

Setting for Success
Have all tools ready to assemble the recipe (bowls, measuring utensils, baking pans, etc.). Before members arrive, you might want to have the recipe prepared correctly so they can taste what the outcome *should* taste like.

Team Theme Talk
Have each person show the item they brought. Ask if anyone would eat this item by itself, just the way it is (raw egg, salt, soda, etc.). Explain that alone, the ingredients do not fulfill their purpose. Just as each team member is more fulfilled when mixing her talents with those of the rest of the team.

Next, hand out a copy of the recipe to each person. Begin mixing the cake and ask for each member's contribution as needed. While adding each ingredient, explain its purpose. If an ingredient is missing because someone is absent or forgot it, leave it out. *The idea is to show the importance of each team member's contribution to the team's accomplishments.* The result of this recipe will depend on who came to the meeting and fulfilled the assignment.

Boiling Water and Quick Oats: These two ingredients need to work together in this recipe. The quick oats (which along with the flour are part of the "foundation" of the cake) need to be cooked to give this cake a moist, firm texture. Without the *boiling* water (warm or cold won't work) and waiting for 20 min, the oatmeal would not have the right feel. Do you feel like you're in "hot water" in your business? Use these experiences to "soften" and teach you.

Oil: In baking, oil is used to tenderize cakes. As part of a team, being tender means listening to and learning from other team members.

Eggs: These have more than one function, depending on what needs

Recipe for Success

to be accomplished. In a cake, eggs give structural support bringing other ingredients together. Eggs also bind items in meatballs and meatloaves together. What can team members do to add support to each other and promote bonding?

Sugars: These are the sweeteners! What kinds of deeds can team members do to add sweetness, goodness, kindness to the team?

Flour: This ingredient is the basis for most recipes. The "flour" of a team represents its members--or base. Just as different types of flours exist for specific tasks, team members can also vary in their interests, participation, and talents. Identify individual talents.

Soda: A leavening agent, soda causes batter or dough to rise and become light and porous. Discuss activities to make business rise.

Cinnamon: A fragrant, well-identified spice, cinnamon adds the flavor to whatever it is combined with. What kind of spice, seasoning, or flavoring can be added to create a wonderfully-selling team?

Frosting: This is not a necessary part of a cake; however, the addition increases the appearance, and more importantly, the taste! What can we top our team with to create a desire to taste, and join?

Activity

This activity is done in conjunction with the Team Talk.

Applause Awards

Leavening Award: For the person who has risen above challenges that have been faced. Use a can of baking powder as the reward

Touch of Spice Award: For the person who has added extra enthusiasm (spice) to the team. Give some spices.

Frosting on the Cake Award: Award the person who has added extra sales, recruits, or activities not normally expected or performed.

Challenge

Because each team member is a very important ingredient to the team, have each one decide what their role and responsibility will be to promote the growth of the team until the next meeting.

Food for Thought

Serve the recipes that were made. First, bake the cake with only the items that were brought. Have everyone taste it. Then, serve the one prepared ahead of time. Ask which tastes the best.

Outstanding Oatmeal Team Cake

1 1/2 cup boiling water   1 cup quick-cooking oats
Combine and let stand 20 minutes.
1/2 cup vegetable oil   1 cup brown sugar   1 cup white sugar
                       2 beaten eggs
Blend until creamy and then add the oat mixture.
Combine and add the following to above:
1 1/3 cup flour   1 tsp. cinnamon   1 tsp. baking soda
Bake in a greased 9 x 13 pan at 350 for 30 minutes.
Frosting:
1 cup brown sugar   1 stick butter   4 Tablespoons milk
Combine all in a saucepan. Bring to rolling boil; add 1/2 cup coconut and 1/2 cup nuts.

Pop Into Action

Objective	*To teach team members that in order to make something happen, prompt action must occur. In other words, they must POP into action--like popcorn in hot oil.*
Invitation *Hand Out*	Print the invitation and attach a zip-top plastic bag of unpopped popping corn or a bag of microwave popcorn.
Bring Along	Request each person bring her own can or bottle of soda pop.
Setting for Success	As team members enter, have popcorn popping in the microwave or on top of a stove. When they enter the room, they will be captivated by the smell of hot, buttered popcorn!
Team Theme Talk	Have you ever asked someone to "motivate" you? Do you have leads you are waiting to call until it's "the right" time? Are you excited about current promotions but don't know where to begin--so you don't?

Have a display of an unpopped kernel of popcorn, one half cup of kernels, and a big bowl of the hot, buttered popcorn. Explain that we are all like this kernel, full of potential! What took these kernels (show unpopped corn) to this (big bowl of popcorn)?

Did the kernel have a written goal that said, "I will become a big, fluffy, piece of popcorn?" Did it read this goal 20 times a day? Did it say, "I'm going to have a positive attitude and then I will turn into popcorn that everyone wants!" Or, maybe it listened to motivational tapes every day. Of course all these ideas can help us pop up a big business, but the key activity of the kernel was *popping into action.*

What caused the kernel to pop? Heat and hot oil. What is the heat and hot oil that will cause you to pop into action? Usually it is having a goal, keeping focused and then *moving--popping--into action!* After a kernel is popped, it is pretty and tasty, but it is all by itself. When a cupful of kernels is popped, the product is a huge bowl of fluffy goodness. But this is just the beginning.

What enhances the flavor of the snack? Butter, salt, other flavorings, and sometimes, gooey syrup! In our business, bringing someone along with us as we Pop Into Action, makes the adventure more fun and profitable! Once we've reached our goal and are developed into a

Pop Into Action

full kernel, we should add more flavoring or seasoning so customers and new recruits will be attracted to us. Create new ways of finding customers by doing something different and unique. Buttered popcorn is great, but gooey, caramel is a different twist that creates more interest.

Remember, many people go through their heat and hot oil without developing into anything different. They remain a hard, small kernel without a future. Do all you can--POP into action--to develop your fullest, most creative potential which in turn brings you profits and prosperity!

Activity

Write as many of the following "POP" words on individual index cards as you want. Have one pile for "P" words and one for the "O"s. Turn the cards, word side down. Go around the room; have each person choose a word from each pile. See what kinds of positive phrases can be created. Team members may have to join with others to create their own "POP Into Action Phrases."

performance	profits	plans	prosperity
passion	peace	participation	power
persistence	perfection	presentation	panorama
professional	picture	progress	please
people	patient	pay	persuade
offer	organize	open	originates
orchestrates	objective	observe	occasion
opinion	opportunity	optimism	order
others	ornament	outstanding	own
over	options	obtain	occupy

Applause Awards

Choose two to three adjectives from the POP game and honor members with those attributes (organized, optimistic, professional, etc.).

Challenge

Using the words from the Activity, have each person choose attributes or action words and commit to POP them into action. (I will *open* my mouth and *offer* my *outstanding, positive-paying opportunity.*)

Food for Thought

Serve the soda pop that everyone brought along with popcorn. For variety, serve flavored popcorns as well.

J.A.M. Session

Objective   To teach members the value of what can be accomplished in **J**ust **A** **M**inute and to open their eyes to many tasks that can be done when they didn't think they had the time.

Invitation
Hand Out   From a restaurant or restaurant supply store, purchase small tubs of jams and jellies. Include one of these with the written invitation.

Bring Along   Request each person to bring their favorite type of jam (a new, unopened jar) to the meeting.

Setting for Success   As team members arrive with the jars of jam, attach or write a number on the bottom or the label. Create a display with these jars. If you are a bread baker (or have an automatic bread maker), you could also have bread baking so the wonderful aroma welcomes everyone as they arrive.

Team Theme Talk   At the beginning of the meeting, announce that you are going to time one minute, **J**ust **A** **M**inute. Without looking at watches, ask team members to raise their hand when they think one minute has lapsed. Have one team member write next to each person's name the number of seconds/minutes when each raised her hand. Then, proceed with the meeting.

Announce the theme: Just a minute - **J.A.M. Session!**

How much time do we waste waiting for food to cook in the microwave, while we're on hold, waiting to pick up kids or during a TV commercial? What home and business activities can we do in just 60 seconds that will make a difference throughout the day??

While we've been taught to "save time," that really is not possible, because we are always spending it--no matter what activities we are involved with.

Let's discuss how to twist time wasters into time makers.

Chapter Seven   *Totally Terrific Team Themes*   *Christie Northrup*

J.A.M. Session

Have team members tell some tasks that could take about 60 seconds. *Business:* open mail, write a thank you note, write a check, put postage on invitations, answer an e-mail, file a folder, "sixty-second" call to encourage or thank a hostess, customer, or other team member...

Personal: wipe off counters or table, clean front of appliances, sweep under the table, make a bed, clean a sink, put dishes away, dust a table, straighten magazines, make sandwiches, tie a shoe, give a compliment, share a hug, smile...

Activity

Use a glass (or any see-through material) jar or bowl. Ask team members to tell you what activities they need to do in a day. For each activity that takes longer than ten minutes, add a raspberry or blueberry to the bowl. For activities that take over ten minutes, add a large strawberry. For all the activities discussed in this meeting (those that take just a few minutes), add small spoonfuls of sugar. This illustrates that "big tasks" can take up a lot of our day, but when we fill in the spaces with the *JAM* tasks, much more can be accomplished. After all suggestions are made, stir the sugar and the fruit together to create "*JAM*" (purchase box of fruit pectin; follow directions for jam). Serve this fruit with a variety of breads or pound cake.

Applause Awards

Use the *JAM* acronym to come up with ideas for recognition and rewards. Here are some ideas:
Jiffy Angel of Motivation: A person who encourages others.
Jolly Acting Magician: Someone who magically inspires others.
Juggle Alot Manager: Great time manager
Job Agent for Millions: Consistent recruiter

Challenge

Write numbers on small pieces of paper corresponding with the number of people in attendance who brought jam. Each person draws a number and matches it to the corresponding number on a jar of jam. The challenge is to take the jam home, use it, and remember that a lot can be accomplished in **Just A Minute!**

Food for Thought

Serve the fruit used in the Activity section with bread or cake.

Create A Beautiful Business

Objective — Using the concept of a "make over" team members will learn how to make over parts of their business that need improvement.

Invitations
Hand out — Purchase candy lipsticks at novelty or dollar shops and attach the meeting information. For added impact on the mailed invitation, use lipstick to draw the outline of lips.

Bring Along — Ask everyone to bring their favorite beauty or woman's magazine that has beauty tips, pictures, and ideas for an appearance transformation.

Setting for Success — Get some before/after pictures of beauty make-overs. Display them around the room to show the differences. A selection of makeup to go along with Team Talk is also helpful. If you know a beauty or skin care consultant, ask if she has small samples you can purchase as gifts or handouts. This will help promote her product too, and can open the door for future cross promoting.

Team Theme Talk — Using Beauty items, liken the tools used for a Beauty make-over to the tools of a business make-over:

Hair: One of the major parts of a make-over is a haircut. Is there something in your business that needs to be cut? How about cutting out procrastination, discouragement, jealousy, complaints, and anything else that weighs down and distracts from a beautiful business.

Cleanse: Make up cannot be applied until the skin is clean. Daily cleansing is crucial in a beauty regime. What daily activities must be accomplished to keep a business clean? Daily contact with customers, potential and current hostesses, sales leader and team members. Making a few calls every day is usually easier than cramming everything into the end of the week.

Foundation: Makeup foundation is like the artist's canvas on a painting. Get a good match and apply as a base. The base of your business is your goal, or the reason you're in business. If you don't have this foundation, the makeup (everything else you do) will not set as nicely.

Eyes: Eyes are your window to the world and the window through which the world sees in to you. What are you looking for in your business? Are you keeping your eyes open for new business all the time? Are you looking for the good in others and in all situations?

Create A Beautiful Business

Blush: This adds color to your complexion. What are you doing to add color to your business? Do you plan and hold fun, informative demonstrations? Do you have product and company knowledge?

Brushes: These are important tools in applying make up correctly. Are you using all your business tools to make your business beautiful. Do you take advantage of all company and local promotions by keeping in touch with your customers? Do you use business-building tools such as literature? What other tools are available?

Lipstick: Lipstick is a very noticeable product. What kinds of words are coming across your lips? Are these words what people want to hear (compliments, information)?

Earrings: More valuable than what you say, is how you listen to your customers, hostesses and team members. As you listen, you'll realize how you can assist them with their situations and in meeting their goals.

Activity

Using the ideas from the beauty magazines, have team members adapt the tips to creating beauty in their business. For example, if a tip suggests outlining lips with a lip pencil so lipstick doesn't smear, ask how that can be adapted to a business make over. Answers could include outlining a day with a plan so time isn't wasted.

Applause Awards

Model Consultant - Award to person who has excelled in many areas of the business: sales, meeting attendance, recruiting, etc.

Make Over of the Month - This goes to the team member who really has made her business over, someone who has created a real transformation

Cover Girl - Highlight someone for something not normally recognized such as highest attendance at demonstrations, most unique ideas, etc.

Challenge

Each member is to choose one aspect of today's team talk and focus on creating more beauty in her business. If she chooses to listen better, have her cut out pictures of ears from the magazine she brought. Make a collage on construction paper as a reminder. If her goal is to add more color, create the collage out of pictures using make up to add color.

Food for Thought

Create mini fruit pizzas. Use large sugar cookies and spread with vanilla pudding. Cut up fruit to resemble parts of faces and let each person create their own beautiful masterpiece.

Putting the Pieces Together

Objective To teach team members how to combine, and sometimes separate, home responsibilities and business tasks so that a near-perfect picture of both areas of life results.

Invitation
Hand Out In addition to the printed invitation, include a puzzle piece from an easy-to-assemble puzzle.

Bring Along Each member brings the puzzle pieces included in their invitations.

Setting for Success As people arrive, have a fun jigsaw puzzle out on a table that they can be putting together until the meeting begins. Also have two or three easy puzzles (fewer than 20 pieces). This will illustrate a point to make in the Challenge section. One of these puzzles could be from the puzzle pieces sent out with the invitations and brought to the meeting.

Team Theme Talk One main reason you might have begun your business is so that you could work from home while building a business and providing a good income for your family. This could be a "perfect picture."

Perhaps the greatest challenge of a home-based business is working to mesh family and business responsibilities and tasks without neglecting either. The first step in combining these two is to realize *sometimes they need to be separated.* While most home-based business owners agree that "family comes first," at times business tasks might take precedence. Many times we try to create one "picture perfect puzzle" from pieces of two different puzzles. Nothing results but chaos! On the other hand, many times both can be united! The answer is in determining what needs to be separated and what can be combined. Ask the group to make three lists: activities for home only, those solely for business, and what can be combined. Here are some ideas:

Home Activities: eating meals together, reading stories, personal one-on-one conversations, kids/spouse returning home from school/work, or other times when family members need your full attention.

Putting the Pieces Together

Business Activities: attending sales meetings, doing individual or group presentations, opportunity interviews, conventions, some telephone calls or anytime your customers need your full attention.

Activities that can be combined: running business and personal errands (meeting customers at sports events or while grocery shopping,) doing household and business tasks (have laundry going while you're doing office tasks; talking on the phone while cooking dinner), busy work involving no personal contact (filing, preparing literature, packing product, folding clothes, etc.)

Activity

Using the puzzles used in "Setting for Success," have one puzzle represent the home responsibilities that should be separated from business. The next puzzle is just the opposite; business tasks that should be separated from home. Try to put the wrong pieces in the wrong puzzle tray to show the difficulties encountered when combining unlike things. The jigsaw puzzle represents the items that can be combined. Doing the separate tasks isn't as difficult as combining, but the final pictures can be works of art! Remind team to remember we can combine our business with family as long as we know when to separate the two.

Applause Awards

Applause Awards go to everyone who brought back the puzzle piece that was included in the invitation. Recognize each of them for being part of the whole team picture. Use the pieces to create the puzzle. If you did not use the "Bring Along" idea, use different pieces of a puzzle as awards and choose recipients accordingly:
Corner Piece: Someone who has been the "cornerstone" of the team, perhaps the person with most longevity.
Connecting Pieces: This award will honor everyone in attendance who has ever sponsored a new person in the business.

Challenge

One big help in meshing a business with family is to make "to do" lists. If our "to dos" become too lengthy, we tend to give up. Just as putting together a 50 piece puzzle is easier than a 1000 piece jig saw, keeping life simpler is easier! Suggest that each team member write down the top 10 things that must be accomplished in a typical day-- business or personal. As the tasks are accomplished, she'll see the pieces come together.

Food for Thought

Serve pizzas. However, instead of slicing into wedges (order them unsliced), cut into puzzle shapes.

We are Number One!

Objective — To teach team members that everything begins with just **one**-- one idea, one goal, one person, and so on. Everything grows from **one** and everything begins with **one**. As team members meet their own individual "*one*" goals, the team will rank **number one** above all others.

Invitation
Hand Out — Attach *one* of an item to each invitation such as *one* page of your product catalog, *one* piece of a package of gum, *one* penny--anything that illustrates this item is simply part of a bigger set/item.

Bring Along — Request each team member bring **one** of something to begin building their business: one customer name, one product to demonstrate, one recruit lead, one order, and so on.

Setting for Success — From a teacher or party supply store, purchase different sizes, shapes, and colors of the number "1". Hang around the meeting room.

Team Theme Talk — In a past-popular song, we heard "one is the loneliest number." However, everything had to start with *one*. So, *one* might be lonely, but it is the *beginning* of everything!

The wonderful thing about *one*, is when it is multiplied by any number other than itself (or zero), it becomes that number (one multiplied by seven becomes seven and so on). So, we must begin with *one*, even though we want more. *One* is the **most powerful number!**

An illustration in nature is a plant that began with *one* seed. Then, that *one* plant bears many, many pieces of fruit or vegetables, which in turn can feed thousands.

In today's technology world, typing in *one* incorrect letter will prevent getting to a website or e-mail address. *One* wrong turn can lead to a disastrous destination.

One person scheduling *one* demonstration leads us to meet several people who we can help by sharing our ideas and products. If just *one* of those guests schedules another demonstration, you have the opportunity to meet another group of several new customers.

We are Number One!

This life line of *one* will lead you to *thousands* of customers, hostesses, and recruits.

As individuals we are only *one,* but we possess the power to influence *many* people. Through demonstrations to a group, we might share *one* idea that helps *one* person find a solution to a situation. Or, by sharing your opportunity with just *one* person, you can change the lives of thousands!

Have you ever greatly benefited from just *one* idea? The company you are a part of most likely began because some*one* had *one* idea or thought. Think what a difference *one* idea of yours can make!

Whenever you feel that you don't make a difference, or that the *one* phone call, or *one* contact with some*one* won't matter, think again! *One is the most important number!*

Activity Have each person think of some*one* who has had a great impact on their life. This could be *one* leader, customer, hostess, friend, parent, etc. If time allows, have each *one* share *one* way that they benefitted from that *one* person. This will continue to show the powerful influence of *one*.

Applause Awards *Onederful Award:* This would be a fun award to give to every*one!* You can site specific examples of why each individual is *one*derful! *Power of One Award:* This is an appropriate award for someone who knew very few people and has grown a significant business, thus demonstrating how important each customer is, even if you only know *one!*

Challenge To take the "one" business-building item they brought and see how many times they can multiply it this month. If they brought "one" order, how many more can they get.

Food for Thought You can use just *one* bottle of soda for a drink, and *one* of something that can be cut into pieces such as pizza, pie or cake. This demonstrates that just as *one* can be multiplied for growth, *one* can also grow through division and sharing (recruiting). This is how individual and team goals are met.

The Lemon Aid Lady   Totally Terrific Team Themes   Chapter Ten

20/20 Vision

Objective — *To teach team members they will see their business and profits more clearly when they focus on a goal. The blurry and fuzzy confusion will turn into clear profits when a goal is achieved. The answer is in 20/20.*

Invitation
Hand Out — Include a pair of plastic sunglasses with the invitation, or glue some "eyes" found at a craft store on the invitation.

Bring Along — Request that each team member bring a pair of glasses to the meeting. This can be their own that they currently wear, an old pair, someone else's glasses, some sun glasses, or a set of drinking glasses (everyone's perception is different!).

Setting for Success — As members arrive, have them put the glasses they brought on display (as long as they don't need them to see).

Team Theme Talk — Perfect vision is considered 20/20. While no "perfect" business exists, we continually strive to make each day better. The best way is to get into focus and make our goals clear. Then, not only does the picture get clearer, our vision is *open* to bigger and better goals and ideas.

What is your vision of what you want to achieve in the next 20 days/ 20 weeks/20 months/20 years?

Just like in planning a trip, decide your destination first--where do you want to be in 20 years? To begin your journey, work backwards. Where do you want to be in 20 months (just a little over a year and a half)? What about in the next 20 weeks--just about a third of a year? What will you be doing in the next 20 days?

Twenty years seems like a long way off; that's how horizons are. Then before you know it, the time has come and gone. Decide now to keep the vision of your destination alive. It begins with today. Spend at least 2 minutes a day looking over what you did, 20 minutes a week, 2 hours a month "polishing" your vision. As you do, your

20/20 Vision

vision becomes clearer. These evaluation periods are like cleaning your glasses every day. About once a year, you usually have your eyes examined; sometimes you need a new prescription. That's where your evaluations come in. Your clear vision might lead you to another goal, in a different direction. It's okay to change the goal just like it's okay to get new glasses, contacts, or even laser surgery to correct poor eyesight. The concept is to check, examine, and correct to get your vision and goals clear!

Activity This activity will show that while we are working on keeping our own vision and goals clear, others on our team and in our life will have their own view, and we have to appreciate and understand that their goals are not our goals and vice versa. Have team members exchange glasses. Can they see out of someone else's? Most likely not. This is why setting our own goals for our own future, not for someone else's is so important.

Applause Awards Have a "fashion show" with the glasses and members can vote (or leader decides) on categories for winners. Biggest frames, oldest, newest, strongest prescription, etc.
Award someone who has worn glasses the longest, least amount, those with bifocals, contacts, etc. Hand out play magnifying glasses to the winners.

Challenge Strive for clearer 20/20 vision by using the 20/20 concept as a challenge. Just as lenses are ground for individual prescriptions, have each person customize the 20/20 challenge to fit their personal vision. Make 20 calls a day for 20 days; make 20 calls in 2 days; do 20 calls in 20 days; hold 20 events in two weeks; 20 events in 20 days, and so forth.

Food for Thought Serve items like cookies, cupcakes, vegetables or anything you can serve in groups of 20.

The Magic of Doubling

Objective — *To teach team members that when efforts are increased, results are often multiplied many times over.*

Invitation Hand Out — Give two invitations to put the "double" in their mind. Two of everything! Mail one out and send the second a while later. You can attach some "double" items such as "double stuff Oreos," "double bubble gum," etc.

Bring Along — Ask everyone to bring a calculator.

Setting for Success — To illustrate the magic of doubling, have a big black hat (like a magician's). Inside put a penny, a fake check for $10,737,418.24 and a calculator. Also have play money or a fake check for $25,000. Use these items at the appropriate times during Team Theme talk.

Team Theme Talk — Present your team with a hypothetical situation: They can each choose a one-time cash bonus of $25,000 (show a fake check or play money), or one penny which will be doubled in value every day for 30 days. At the end of the 30 days, they will get the amount that has been accumulated. What would each of them choose? For the greatest yield, the correct answer is the penny. At the end of thirty days, a penny doubled every day has a value of $5,368,709.12. Add that to the daily accumulated totals and the value is $10,737,418.24.

There is magic in *doubling*. Wherever you are now, decide to have double sales, growth, recruiting, booking, etc. in the next period.

How do you begin? By doing and believing! Dissect the word "*double.*" It begins with "DO." The next part, "U" and the BLE stands for "you believe." "Do you believe?" If you do, you are ready to begin. The magic part is that in the beginning, you might put in double the effort, and see small results--much like this magic penny. The penny was only worth $81.92 by day 14!

Chapter Twelve *Totally Terrific Team Themes* *Christie Northrup*

The Magic of Doubling

After a while, you can get double results without double the effort. For example, have you ever doubled a recipe for cookies? Did mixing the batch up take twice as long? Usually not. Do you ever get "double prints" when having your film developed? Did you have to shoot twice the amount of film? No. Getting double the results does not have to take double the amount of time, but it will take extra effort.

Recruiting is a wonderful example of the magic of doubling. When we add double the amount of people by recruiting, the end results are typically more than double!

Activity — Using the calculators that everyone brought (have some available as well), make a chart about the magic penny. Have 30 lines on a sheet of paper. First line is .1, second is .2, and so forth until day 30 which is $4,368,709.12. Decide as a group what kinds of activities can be doubled during the next sales period.

Applause Awards — *Double Digit Achievers* - For everyone who held or scheduled 10 or more sales events, gave 10 or more referrals, had events with 10 or more guests, etc.
Double the Pleasure, Double the Profits - Give an award to whomever doubled activity (sales events held, contacts made, dollars sold, etc.) from the period before. This is great for members who are just beginning because doubling smaller numbers is easier than larger numbers.

Challenge — Team members can "chews" their "magic of doubling" challenge (this will double their sales/profits/activity):
--double sales/activities from the previous period
--be a double digit performer in events held, scheduled, etc.
--double themselves by recruiting someone
Hand out sticks of Double Mint gum as a reminder.

Food for Thought — Double Dip Ice Cream Cones and/or
Double Decker Sandwiches (sandwiches with three slices of bread and two layers of filling)

I Love My Business

Objective — To teach team members the importance of being in love with their business. Maintaining a love affair with a business is similar to human relationships; it takes time and effort to build and bind.

Invitation
Hand Out — Include a box of conversation hearts or heart-shaped candy with the invitation.

For those being mailed out, decorate with heart stickers.

Bring Along — A list with seven reasons why the team member loves her business. These reasons should be very specific to be meaningful. For example, instead of writing, "I get to work out of my home," write, "My daughter was playing dolls and pretended to be me doing my business. It was gratifying to see her copying me and enjoying what she was doing."

Setting for Success — Create a romantic atmosphere by decorating room with wedding photos and invitations, romance novels and magazines, flowers, etc. Have soft rock music playing in the background.

Team Theme Talk — Remember how you felt when you first decided to join the business? Everything looked great; you were so excited to sell and to excel! And you did. After a while, when your enthusiasm dwindled, so did your sales, and vice versa. You wonder, "What is wrong?" Probably nothing. However, knowing the stages we all go through in a business helps us understand where we are and to decide the stage in which we want to remain. Understanding the stages is easier when we compare them to the stages of a love relationship.

Flirting: You've heard about the business opportunity and are very intrigued! You attend an opportunity meeting or maybe a demonstration to find out more. However, you're still fickle and continue to look at other companies. You look at things from a short-term point of view rather than long-term vision. You're looking at a business mostly for the fun, not serious about building a career.

Dating: While you continue to "play the field," you've joined a company but continue to keep your eyes open looking for something that promises to be better. You don't want to make any long-term commitments.

I Love My Business

Engagement: You've finally found *the one and only!* You are becoming more committed. You seek more education on your product and industry. You are planning and looking toward the future in you company!

Honeymoon: This is the stage most people advance to quickly after deciding to join a company. You are completely in love with your business, nothing can go wrong. You overlook any faults either in your leader, company, or co-workers. You have big, optimistic plans for the future, nothing is going to hold you back! Business is great!

Happily Ever After: The honeymoon might be over, but you celebrate your business every day! Your pledge for "richer and poorer" remains intact. Yes, there are "those days," when you want to give up at times, but you remember your commitment and know that in order to progress to the "golden years," you will learn from your challenges and grow stronger from trials. You're committed to this relationship!

Activity

Fill a bowl with candy conversation hearts. Have each person take a handful. Then, ask each to write a sentence with the hearts that describes how they feel about their business. They can share hearts with other members, if they need/want to.

Applause Awards

Persons in the Flirting/Dating Stage: This will recognize all the recruit-type guests in attendance. Encourage them to progress and decide to make a commitment to the business.
Golden Years Award: Recognize one or more persons with longevity in the business.
Additional Awards: If desired, recognize each person for the stage they are in (have each person tell what stage she is in).

Challenge

Just as personal relationships grow with praise and falter with criticism, so do any relationships, including business. Challenge the team to keep a personal "love journal" by daily adding to their list of seven reasons why they are in love with their business. Watch their business and recruiting blossom!

Food for Thought

Serve something reminiscent of romance such as heart-shaped cakes or cookies, or anything chocolate.

My Business is a Picnic

Objective To have an informal group meeting and celebrate each other and the fun business. This is an appropriate meeting to invite the families of the group to attend and to involve them in support and recognition.

Invitation Hand Out Attach small packets of ketchup or mustard to the written invitation. To add interest to the invitation, use a fine-tip point ketchup and/or mustard bottle and outline the word "ketchup" on the front of the invitation. Let it sit overnight to dry.

Bring Along A potluck food assignment.

Setting for Success A park is the perfect setting for this event.

Team Theme Talk Using the analogy of picnic items, discuss ways to build a team.
Food: Picnic usually means food! You can have food without a picnic, but you cannot have a picnic without food! The food of your business is the product. Your company probably has a banquet of products. Some people want everything; others are more choosy. Each person has different tastes and appetites. A team member's role is to provide the appropriate food--or product--for the customer to choose.
Drinking Cups: Quench your customers' thirst by creating a desire to own and use your product. Use word pictures and examples. Help them to visualize themselves using and owing your product or joining your team!
Plates: A lot of yummy food is served at picnics. An item to put the food on is very necessary! Plates are the ideas you share with your products. If you don't show the features and benefits and relate them to your customers needs, your customer will starve by not purchasing anything--so will you because you won't have an income!
Utensils (knives, forks, spoons): We can eat some, but not all foods with fingers. However, using utensils makes eating easier and cleaner. The utensils are the service you provide your customers with. They could purchase your product without your service, but it wouldn't last for long!

My Business is a Picnic

Seasonings (salt and pepper): Season food with salt and pepper or other seasonings. This isn't necessary, but the flavor of the food is enhanced. What are you doing to enhance what you offer your customers? New ideas, extra service, etc.?

Tablecloth: Another non-essential, but helpful item. This represents your demonstrations. People like to see products and how they are to be used, just as they like to have a nice covering on their tables.

Matches: If you plan to cook your food, you usually need a match to light the fire. This is one item many picnickers forget! Your match is your love and enthusiasm for your product and company!

Picnic Basket: When we go on a picnic, many items are needed to make a picnic memorable and enjoyable. A container for carrying these tools is helpful. You are like picnic baskets to their customers. You bring everything together and help serve them so they keep their life in order!

Activity

Provide (or assign) ingredients for the team and their families to create their own Big MAC Cookies. This stands for My Awesome Company or Morning After Calls (or come up with something else you want MAC to stand for).

You'll need: Vanilla wafer cookies (hamburger bun), round chocolate-covered mint candies (hamburger), white, yellow, and/or red frosting (mayo, mustard, catsup), green colored coconut (lettuce). Each person assembles own "Big MAC". The frostings you choose is what holds everything together.

Applause Awards

Promote this event a month or two ahead of time. Recognize and reward top performers in sales, activities and recruits with a *TWIST*: when a team member qualifies for recognition and reward, give this to her child and have kid-related items for gifts. When you announce this ahead of time, the kids will encourage and push their parent to success so they will get the reward. If a person doesn't have a child, she can bring a friend's or relative's. If the team member has more than one child, encourage her to qualify in more than one category.

Challenge

Connect the challenge with the Big MAC activity. Reinforce follow through with Morning After Calls or recruiting by talking about My Awesome Company.

Food for Thought

You'll be feasting on a picnic and friendships during this meeting.

Back to School; Back to Work

Objective
To teach team members going to work everyday is like going to school. The basics of the business are critical to continual learning and growth.

Invitation
Hand Out
Attach meeting information to an inexpensive back-to-school item such as pencils, erasers, notebook.
Invitation is supplied in the back, or you can use black construction paper and write meeting information with white chalk. Let it dry before folding the paper so it doesn't smear.

Bring Along
Request each team member to bring a product to "show and sell".

Setting for Success
As the group enters, have a blackboard or white board with the words "Welcome to Back to School; Back to Work"

Team Theme Talk
Divide into and attend different classes as listed below--just like in high school. These classes can be held in different areas of your meeting room or in separate rooms. Depending on your time, everyone can attend all on a rotating basis, or choose a set number. Suggested length of time per class is 10-15 minutes.

Math: This is the subject to take if you want to multiply recruits. The simple fact is in order to multiply, you must divide by sharing your business opportunity. And, when you divide you multiply (when you share, your business actually grows!) Give some math and recruiting ideas.

Language: In this class, the language of phone techniques will be discussed with both warm and cold leads. Read the **Lemon Aid Lead Alphabet, page 103** for more ideas.

Writing: Provide postcards or note paper to write complimentary notes to someone who has had an influence on the members' business or life. This could be for the sales leader, customer, or co-worker.

Back to School; Back to Work

Reading: Have a mini library of inspirational books. Share ideas from a couple and encourage team members to "check out" the books from you for a short period of time or purchase from a bookstore. Suggested textbooks:

The Greatest Salesman in the World by Og Mandino
How to Win Friends and Influence People by Dale Carnegie
Dig your well Before you're Thirsty by Harvey Mackay
Think and Grow Rich by Napolean Hill
Lemon Aid Books by Christie Northrup, The Lemon Aid Lady:
 Where to Find Customers when you run out of Family and Friends
 The Deeds you need to Lead your Leads to Long-term Customers and Residual Profits

P.E.: Take this class to get your business in shape. Provide a workshop atmosphere for calling customers; past, present, and future! This is a great exercise that must be performed daily.

Activity

Show and Sell - Each person has 60-90 seconds (depending on size of group and time allowed) to do a "Show and Sell" with the item they brought in the "Bring Along" section. Use a school bell and ring when time is up. This is a wonderful way to get to know each other better and learn more product tips.

Applause Awards

Reward "Straight A" Students. Those with outstanding
Attitude: This is presented to the member who keeps moving on in spite of challenges and doesn't complain.
Achievement: Recognize an achievement beyond the usual sales, activity, and recruits. Perhaps the most calls made, demonstrations scheduled, etc.
Attendance: To the person(s) who attend team meetings faithfully.

Challenge

Sales leader can have "report cards" prepared with sales achievement for the past month/quarter/year. Always include something complimentary as well as an area for improvement. Personalize the challenge for each team member. Have them bring the report card to the next team meeting with the challenge results written down.

Food for Thought

Serve graham crackers and milk, or peanut butter and jelly sandwiches. Or, have each "student" bring a sack lunch.

Them Bones!

Objective — This is a fun Halloween theme meeting; however, it can be used any time to illustrate that our back bone is the most important part of our body and business.

Invitation Hand Out — Around Halloween, look for small "skeleton" novelties such as key chains, stickers, etc. Attach to the invitation.

Bring Along — Ask everyone to bring a bone--a bone that dogs chew on, bone from meat, milk bone dog biscuits, etc.

Setting for Success — Hang Halloween skeletons around the room.

Team Theme Talk — We have all kinds of bones in our bodies; each has its purpose. We'll discuss just four kinds of bones today--Wish Bones, Funny Bones, Jaw Bones, and Back Bones. As you discuss each type use the suggested props.

Wishbone: Show a bottle of Wishbone salad dressing or a wishbone from a chicken or turkey. Ask how many are "wishbones?" We set contest or sales goals, map out what it takes to achieve them, and then stop. We believe because we have made the plan, our goal will be achieved. Nothing will happen until your wishes are put to work.

Funny Bone: Get some dog chew bones from the butcher. Cover with the colored comic pages from the Sunday newspaper. Acknowledge that humor is an important part of life. It entertains and lightens our load, it is effective in teaching as well. However, some people try just to be funny to cover up for lack of knowledge.

Jaw bones: Use jaw breaker candy to illustrate this point. We all need a good jaw bone to communicate. But, are we giving our jaws too much exercise? Do we talk too much and work or listen too little?

Them Bones!

Back Bone People: The back bone in a body keeps a person standing up--hopefully standing straight. This is a strong bone and is not fickle. This type of person is one who is committed, will not stray from goals and is strong in business and life.

Activity

Have five members read through this poem (one the introduction and for each kind of bone) to reiterate what you just taught.

*The bones in the body are two hundred or more,
but for sorting out people, we need only four.*

Wish Bone People
*They hope for, they long for, they wish for and sigh;
The want things to come, but aren't willing to try.*
Funny Bone People
*They laugh, grin, and giggle, smile, twinkle the eye;
If work is a joke, sure, they'll give it a try!*
Jaw Bone People
*They scold, jaw and sputter, they froth, rave and cry;
They're long on the talk, but they're short on the try.*
Back Bone People
*They strike from the shoulder, They're winners in life.
They work hard and regular and live without strife.*

Applause Awards

Strong Bones Award: Determine who has the heaviest purse or appointment planner and needs strong bones to carry them.
Rattle Bones Award: This goes to the person who is still a little nervous about the business and might have "rattle bones" when getting up in front of people.

Challenge

Strengthening the back bone, or in other words, commitment to family, business, and other goals is the basis for this meeting. Hand out a reminder for team members such as Tums (full of calcium for strong bones). Encourage a commitment to commitment by having a strong back bone and not swaying to outside forces.

Food for Thought

If you want to serve a dinner, chicken (with bones, of course) is a good choice. Add other "calcium rich" foods like dark green vegetables and dairy products. For dessert, "chicken bones" candy is very appropriate (coconut-covered candy).

Symbols of the Season

Objective *To tie up the year by associating the symbols of the season with the business opportunity that each consultant enjoys and to encourage them to share these symbols with others outside of the company.*

Invitation
Hand Out

Attach one of the symbols listed below to the written invitation.

Bring Along Request each team member to bring a new Christmas card--not one they have been given--with nothing written on it.

Setting for Success Festively decorate the room for a holiday feeling. Play Christmas music, light fragrant candles, have decorations hung. If desired, hang the Symbols of the Season on a Christmas tree and take each off as they are mentioned in the Team Theme Talk.

Team Theme Talk This Team Theme Talk can be done by the leader, assigned to a team member, or for more participation, assign each symbol to a different member. The leader can do the last one to tie things up. Choose which order to explain the symbols relevant to your company, team, and needs. Not all symbols need to be used.

Tree: Money does not grow on trees, but our business opportunity will teach you how to have a business where money does grow. For an average demonstration of ____ in sales, your profits would be approximately ____. The more demonstrations and customers you have, the more money you will "grow." **Prop:** Small table-top-sized Christmas tree.

Cane: In the beginning, you might be a little wobbly, so my supervisor and I will be your cane. You can count on us to support you! **Prop:** Candy Canes

Cookies: The sweet thing about this business is you can design it however you want. If you want to "frost" your business with full-time income or "sprinkle" it with part-time hours, you decide! You are the decorator and will reap the benefits you design--and desire. **Prop:** Plain sugar cookie. Frost with icing as you present full-time and with sprinkles when talking about part-time options.

Bell: The bell stands for the recognition you'll get when you join our team. We salute you for your efforts and accomplishments--we ring the bell for you! **Prop:** Ring a festive holiday bell as you're doing this presentation.

Symbols of the Season

Season's Colors: Is your checkbook a little in the *red* (spending more money than you have)? Change that color to *green money* as you determine your own income. Your investment for this opportunity is only _____. **Props:** A red pen for deducting debits out of a checkbook, green money which are recruiting dollars (get these by calling the Booster at 1-800-5JENNYB).

Stockings: Gift stockings are full of surprises--so is an opportunity with our company. From monthly promotions to contest gifts to training trips, you'll be delighted with what's in store! **Prop:** A stocking with sample of gifts earned (either the real thing or pictures).

Lights: Every person on our team is important--just like every light on the strand of holiday lights. We need you to brighten our team just as you need us to brighten your life! **Prop:** A strand of Christmas lights with one bulb taken out. Plug them in and show that the strand won't light up without all the sockets filled. Put the missing bulb in the and the strand lights up! This shows the importance of each person and that our team won't shine without the entire team!

Activity

Using the Christmas cards that everyone brought (have extras available), encourage all members to address the card to someone, who they feel, would most benefit from your business opportunity. Attach this card to the item in the Challenge section.

Applause Awards

Ho - Ho Award: Since this is the season to be jolly, give this award to the person who has the "**H**appy **O**ffice, **H**ome **O**ffice." You can announce this the month before so everyone can put their happy smiles on their answering machines and other activities and show they have a *HO HO* attitude!

Challenge

Give each team member a small version of one of the symbols such as a candy cane, small jingle bell, etc. Challenge them to *give this item away* to someone they want to give a greater gift to--a business opportunity. Teach them how to show the receiver what the gift is all about. Include the card from the Activity Section.

Food for Thought

Provide plain sugar cookies in a variety of holiday shapes along with frosting, sprinkles, and other decorating items. Encourage everyone to design their cookies--and their careers this holiday season.

The Lemon Aid Lady   *Totally Terrific Team Themes*   *Chapter Seventeen*

Academy Awards

Objective — To recognize team for star-studded performance. This can be an annual, formal event at the end of the calendar or fiscal year.

Invitation
Hand Out — Attach a fake movie ticket to the invitation or a flyer showing the newest movies or videos available.

Bring Along — Each team member is encouraged to invite a companion: a spouse or friend to celebrate a festive, fun evening of recognition and camaraderie. Just as the Hollywood event, make this a night to dress up in the finest. Consider holding this at a nice restaurant or facility where a dinner could be catered, depending on the team circumstances. If a dinner is part of the event, team members could qualify for their meal to be paid for, everyone else pays for themselves and companions--this is up to the leader.

Setting for Success — In addition to a fancy, festive table setting, you might want to hang movie posters around the room. Use sealed envelopes to announce the winners in each category. As couples arrive, take pictures, just as reporters do at the Oscars.

Team Theme Talk — Because this evening is reserved for recognition, the Team Theme, Applause Awards, and Activities Sections are combined. As the awards are given, a brief explanation can be given and ideas woven in with the significance of the award and how it was achieved. As individuals are honored, their "acceptance speech" can also be a form of educating the rest of the team.

For the trophies, visit novelty and/or trophy stores to see what kinds of "Oscars" are available. Create a name for the trophy that has a connection with your company/product/team. As you do this evening year after year, your trophy will become coveted, just as the Oscars are to film makers.

For the entertainment, assign a couple of team members short presentations about how they grew their business (much like the musical performances that are performed at the Academy Awards).

Academy Awards

Best Lighting: Someone "lights up the room" with her appearance; someone who always wears a smile.

Best Screen Play: The person who is known for doing superior demonstrations.

Best Supporting Actress/Actors: Depending on how many "top" people are recognized will determine how many "supporting cast members" are honored. If you do top ten in sales, nine would be best supporting.

Best Actress/Actor: Top in sales

Best Director(s): This is an honor for those who have moved up the leadership ladder from your team to lead their own teams

Best Producer(s): Those who produced the most recruits

Best Editor: Highest in activities held.

Best Original Score: The person with most/highest fund-raisers.

Peer Award: Just as winners of the Oscars are nominated by peers, create an award for team members to nominate and vote for someone who is the overall "epitome" of a top performer--someone who gave a great performance on and off stage...meaning not only in front of customers but as a team member as well. Have the nominations due a couple of weeks before.

Best Picture: This goes to the team as a whole for creating the picture of success. End with this and everyone leaves feeling fabulous!

Awards for the top performers, just as best actress and actor, will be given last.

Challenge The end of a time period is always a good time to reflect and plan for new goals. Encourage each team member to decide now what awards they want to be recognized for at the next Academy Award evening. To remind people of tonite and of future goals, create a souvenir program listing the winners in each of the above categories.

Food for Thought Serve a fancy dessert or dessert buffet. Perhaps have each team member bring their favorite dessert for the buffet.

TOTALLY TERRIFIC TEAM TREASURES

The following pages are reproducible invitations for your team meetings. Permission is granted to the owner of this book to reproduce these invitations for personal team, non-commercial use.

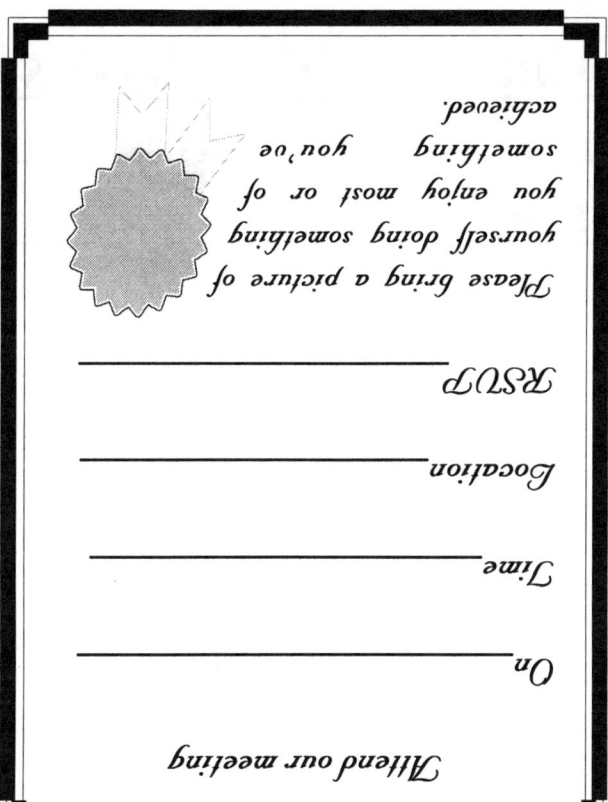

Attend our meeting

On _____

Time _____

Location _____

RSVP _____

Please bring a picture of yourself doing something you enjoy most or of something you've achieved.

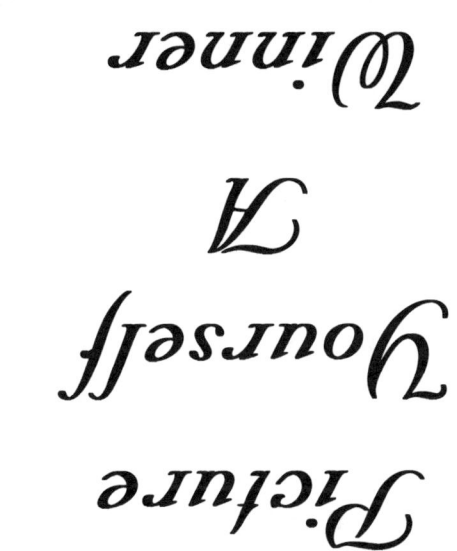

Picture Yourself A Dinner Winner

Feel free to share this
important invitation
with anyone who is serious
about adding more
Sweet Successes
and
Juicy Profits
to their life.

Copyright 1999
Christie Northrup
The Lemon Aid Lady
Dallas, TX 75065
888-358-3001

You are a Winner!

Get the Fax on business-building basics

Attend our team meeting...

To: From:

CC: All team members
Phone number:
Fax number:

❑ Urgent   Date sent:
❑ For Review   Time sent:
❑ Please Comment   Number of pages including cover page:
❑ Please Reply

Message:

Team meeting will be held on _____

Time_____ Location_____

RSVP_____

You will learn basic selling and recruiting skills and get to know other team members.

Please bring one rubber band with you.

 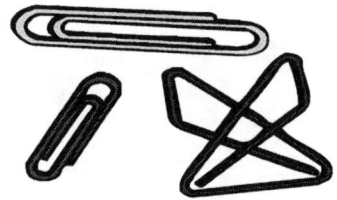 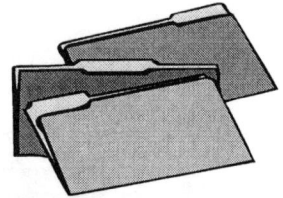

Feel free to pass this important invitation on to anyone who is serious about adding more
Sweet Success and Juicy Profits
to their life.
Copyright 1999 Christie Northrup, The Lemon Aid Lady, Dallas TX 888-358-3001

Join us at Team Meeting

Day/Date _____

Time _____

Location _____

RSVP _____

Please bring a book that has meaning to you to the meeting.

From Terrific Titles To Concrete Content, Learn how to be a Best Seller in the business

Feel free to share this important invitation with anyone who wants to add more
Sweet Successes
and
Juicy Profits
to their life.

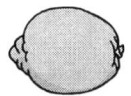

Copyright 1999
Christie Northrup
The Lemon Aid Lady
Dallas, Texas 75065
888-358-3001

Become a Best Seller

If it turns green,
　Call your Dentist.
If it turns blue,
　Call your Chiropractor.
If it turns brown,
　Call your Pharmacist.
If it turns yellow,
　Call your Optometrist.
If it turns pink,
　Call your Obstetrician.

If this paper doesn't change colors after you blow on it,
You are in perfect health and Are able to attend team meeting:

Day/Date_____
Time_____ R.S.V.P._____
Location_____

Learn how to cure diseases that might be making your business ill. Please bring an item from a First Aid Kit.

BLOW ON THIS CARD

Feel free to share this important invitation with anyone who wants to add more
Sweet Successes
and
Juicy Profits
to their life.

Copyright 1999
Christie Northrup
The Lemon Aid Lady
Dallas, Texas 75065
888-358-3001

Recipe for Success

Feel free to share this important invitation with anyone who wants to add more
Sweet Successes
and
Juicy Profits
to their life.

Copyright 1999
Christie Northrup
The Lemon Aid Lady
Dallas, Texas 75065
888-358-3001

Recipe for Success

From the Kitchen of _____

Recipe for: *Outstanding Team and Personal Performance*
Combine the following ingredients in a meeting to be held on:
Day/Date/Time _____
At _____
All team members
Enthusiasm
Desire for fun and profit
Knowledge
Recognition
Simmer for two hours and taste the goodness of team and personal success. Serves all who attend.

Please Bring this important ingredient with you:

Feel free to share this important invitation with anyone who wants to add more
Sweet Successes
and
Juicy Profits
to their life.

Copyright 1999
Christie Northrup
The Lemon Aid Lady
Dallas, Texas
75065
888-358-3001

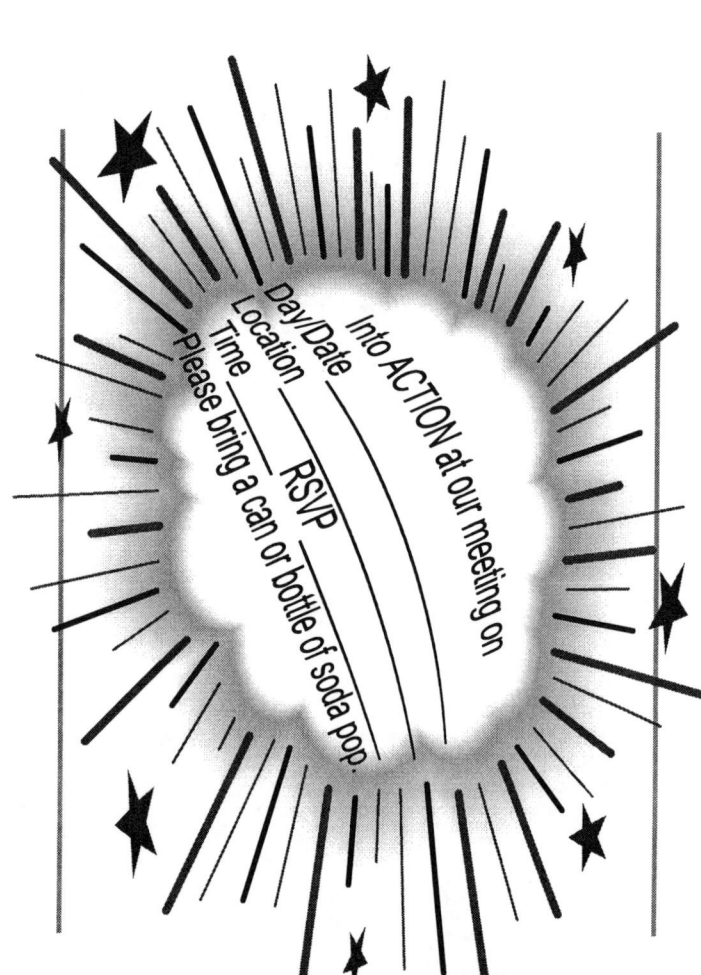

Into ACTION at our meeting on
Day/Date
Location
Time
RSVP
Please bring a can or bottle of soda pop.

Attend our team
J.A.M. SESSION

Date _____ Time _____

Place _____

R.S.V.P. _____ by _____

"Turn Minutes into Memories and Money."

In addition to a recruit-type guest, please bring
A jar of your favorite jam.

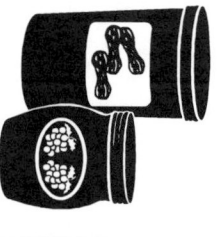

Are you in a Sticky Situation...

because you don't have
time
to get
everything done?

Are you in a Sticky Situation...

Feel free to pass this important invitation on to anyone who is serious about adding *Sweet Successes and Juicy Profits* to their life.

Copyright 1999
Christie Northrup
The Lemon Aid Lady
Dallas, TX 75065
888-358-3001

Create a Beautiful Business

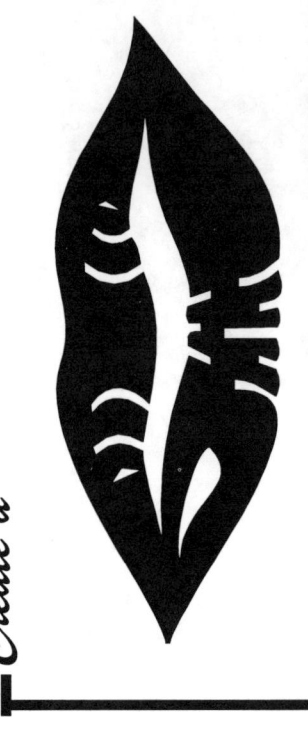

Please bring a Fashion or Woman's Magazine to the meeting.

Attend our meeting to create a Beautiful Business Make Over

Day/Date _____

Time _____ RSVP _____

Location _____

"You'll be talking about this for a long time!"

Feel free to share this important invitation with anyone who is serious about adding more
Sweet Success
And
Juicy Profits
to their life.

Copyright 1999
Christie Northrup
The Lemon Aid Lady
Dallas, TX 75065
888-358-3001

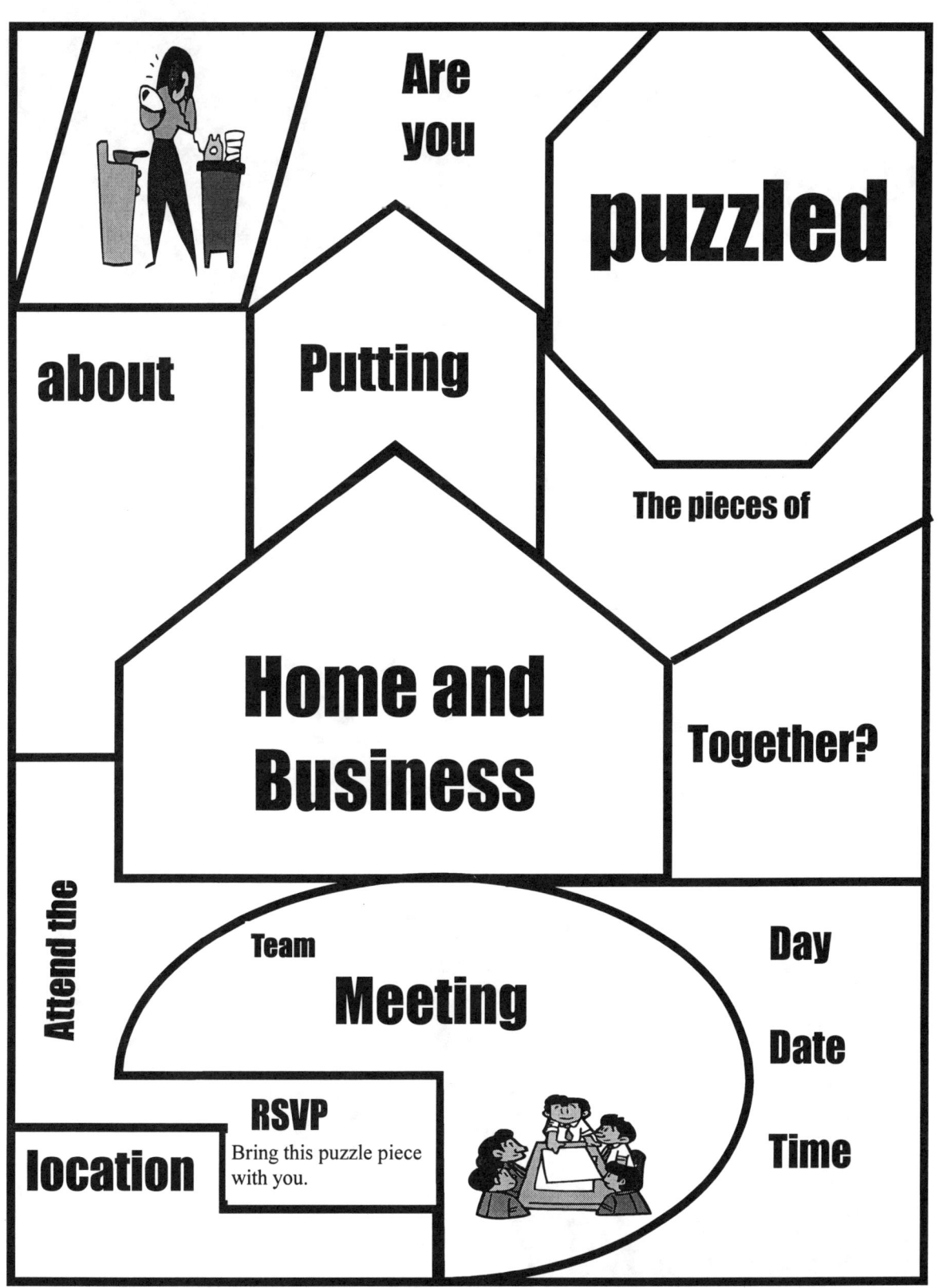

Feel free to share this important invitation with any one you know who wants more Sweet Successes and Juicy Profits in their life.
Copyright 1999 Christie Northrup, The Lemon Aid Lady, Dallas, TX 75065 888-358-3001

S
SEE THE
VISION
ATTEND OUR
MEETING

Day/date_____Time_____

Location_____RSVP_____

Bring a pair of  glasses.

Feel free to share this important information with anyone who wants more Sweet Success and Juicy Profits in their life.

Copyright 1999 by Christie Northrup, The Lemon Aid Lady, Dallas, TX 75065 888-358-3001

Double Double

Double your
Sales sales
Profits profits
Business
Business

Feel free to share this important information with anyone who is serious about doubling
Sweet Success
And
Juicy Profits
in their life.

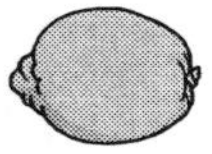

Copyright 1999
Christie Northrup
The Lemon Aid Lady
Dallas, TX 75065
888-358-3001

Details on Doubling
At the meeting:

Day/Date/Time _____

Location _____

RSVP _____

Please bring a calculator with you.

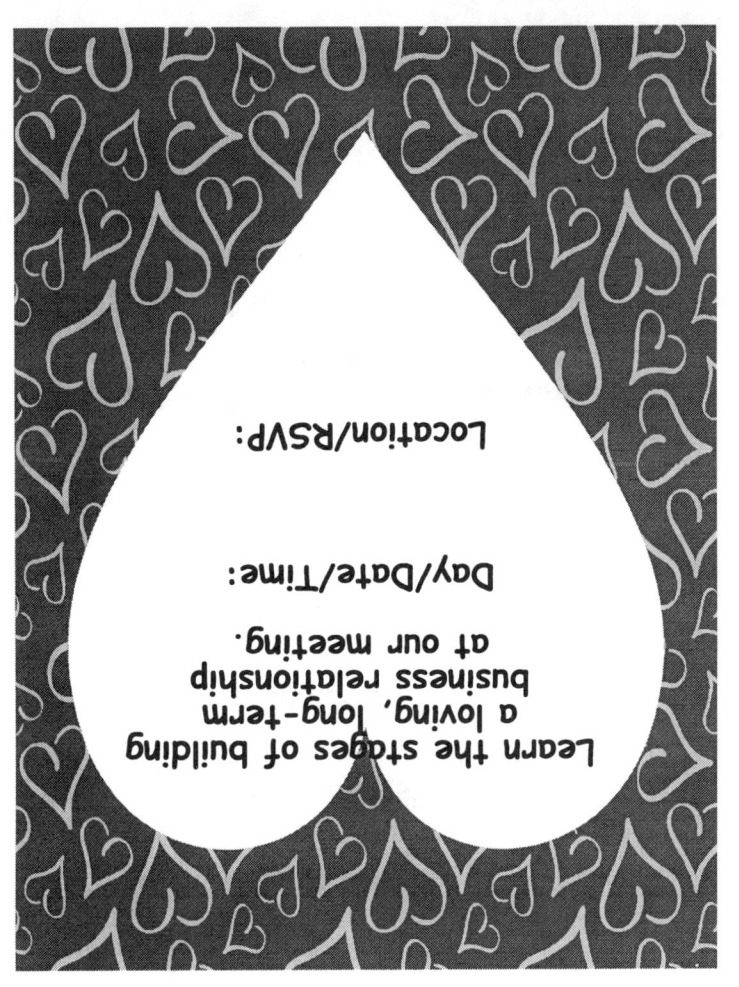

Location/RSVP:

Day/Date/Time:

Learn the stages of building a loving, long-term business relationship at our meeting.

Bring this love list with you.

7.
6.
5.
4.
3.
2.
1.

Let me count the ways...

Feel free to share this important invitation with anyone who wants to add more
Sweet Successes
and
Juicy Profits
to their life.

Copyright 1999
Christie Northrup
The Lemon Aid Lady
Dallas, TX 75065
888-358-3001

How do I love my Business?

Join the
"Hot Dogs"
in our group for
fun, food,
recognition, and recreation.
Your family is invited to attend.
Please bring

You
"mustard"
up so the event will be a
Success!

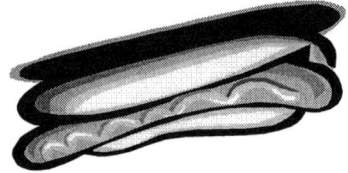

Day, Date, and Time

Location and directions:

Feel free to share this important invitation with anyone who wants to add more
Sweet Success
And
Juicy Profits
to their life.

Copyright 1999
Christie Northrup
The Lemon Aid Lady
Dallas, TX 75065
888-358-3001

LET'S
KETCHUP
ON SOME FUN…

PLEASE BRING A PRODUCT TO SHOW AND SELL

(While the item will not actually be "sold," ideas for showing features and benefits will be discussed.)

Day/ Date _____
Time _____
Location _____
_____
RSVP _____

The more you learn, the more you earn.

Add more class to your business as you learn how to:

⇒ Multiply by dividing
⇒ Exercise for profits
⇒ Read for remarkable results
⇒ Talk in sales language
⇒ Write for the right reason

Feel free to share this important invitation with anyone who wants to add more
Sweet Successes
and
Juicy Profits
to their life.

Copyright 1999
Christie Northrup
The Lemon Aid Lady
Dallas, Texas 75065
888-358-3001

Back to School... Back to Work

ARE YOURS SHAKEY SCAREY OR STRONG? LEARN ABOUT BUSINESS BONES AND WHAT KIND YOU HAVE!

TEAM MEETING

DAY/DATE _____

TIME _____

LOCATION _____

RSVP _____

PLEASE BRING A BONE OR AN ITEM WITH A BONE IN IT.

Feel free to pass this important invitation on to anyone who is serious about creating more
Sweet Success
and
Juicy Profits
in their life.

Copyright 1999
Christie Northrup
The Lemon Aid Lady
Dallas, TX 75065
888-358-3001

THEM BONES!

Please bring a new Christmas card with you.

Day/Date _____

Time _____

Location _____

R.S.V.P.
_____
_____

Symbols of the Season

Symbols of the Season will remind us of the Reason Our Business is something to Celebrate!

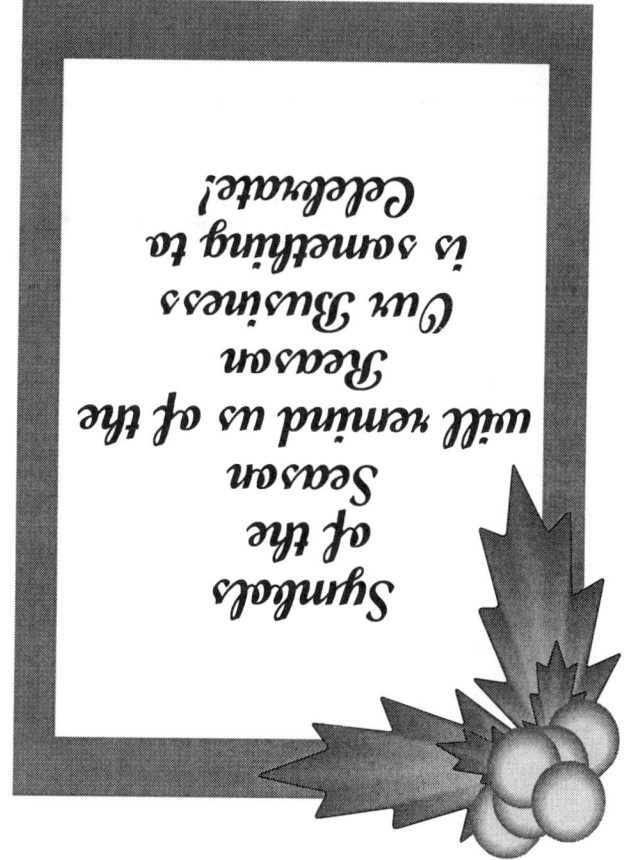

Feel free to share this important invitation with anyone who wants to add more
Sweet Successes
and
Juicy Profits
to their life.

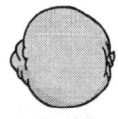

Copyright 1999
Christie Northrup
The Lemon Aid Lady
Dallas, TX 75065
888-358-3001

Symbols of the Season

(upside-down top half:)

At Team Academy Awards Night

Be among the Stars
As we celebrate
Success!

Day/Date _____

Time _____

Location _____

RSVP _____

Feel free to share this important invitation with
anyone who is serious about adding more
Sweet Success
And
Juicy Profits
to their life.

Copyright 1999
Christie Northrup
The Lemon Aid Lady
Dallas, TX 75065
888-358-3001

Please be our guest...

Are you Thirsting for more Hostesses, Customers, and Recruits?

Invite The Lemon Aid Lady to quench that thirst with classes tailored to you...

Lemon Aid Learning Adventures™ now offers a variety of classes...in different formats...to help you book more demonstrations, sell to more customers, and greatly expand your team with new recruits and more leaders.

On-site Classes
We've adapted our popular Lemon Aid Learning Adventures for team meetings. For groups of 50 or more, we'll come to your location with a two-hour presentation custom-tailored to your company, area, and team needs. Call for details.

Team Telephone Talk
If your group is small, take heart! We offer a 45-minute team talk by phone.

Lemon Aid One-on-One
Personal coaching, Lemon Aid style! In personal, half-hour phone sessions, Christie will help you *twist* your personal Sour Situations into Sweet Successes and Juicy Profits.

Three Options. A myriad of topics..
We offer a wide variety of presentations, including:

Sales	Leadership
• Where to Find Customers when you Run out of Family and Friends	• From Parenting Your Team to Mentoring Your Team
• Presentations for Profit$	• Lemon Aid for Leaders
• Family Fortunes without Family Feuds	• Totally Terrific Teams
• There's No Place Like Working From Home	• Opportunity Meetings with a *TWIST*
	• When Life Give You Lemons, Start a Lemon Aid Stand

Lemon Aid Learning Adventures. Creating Sweet Successes and Juicy Profits!

Lemon Aid Learning Adventures
P.O. Box 1720
Lake Dallas TX 75065
940-498-0995   www.lemonaidlady.com

Add more Sweet Successes and Juicy Profits with these other Lemon Aid™ Books and Tapes!

Presentations for Profit$
The demonstration is the backbone of a home-party business. But it's more than just presenting products. In *Presentations for Profits$,* you'll learn dozens of ways to increase your bookings and recruit more hostesses at home party demonstrations through creative preparation, presentation, recognition, and follow-through.
$21.95

The Lemon Aid Lead Alphabet: Where to Find Customers when you run out of Family and Friends
Quench your thirst for new business with the ABCs of generating sales leads. This 115-page book is written in an easy-to-use, reference-style format. No need to read the book from cover to cover. Simply turn to any page for easy, creative, no-cost ideas for finding people who want and need your product or service.
$21.95

The Lemon Aid Deed Alphabet
Once you have located leads, what deeds do you need to do to convert them to committed customers? Written in the same format as the *Lead Alphabet*, this 120-page book will teach you what to do to keep your customers committed to YOU and how to it.
$19.95

Totally Terrific Team Themes
Are your team meetings a treat to plan? Do team members look forward to attending the meetings? Does performance increase after a meeting is held? The answers to all these questions will be a firm "yes" when you plan your meetings using the themes in this book.
$19.95

The Lemon Aid Lead Alphabet Tape Series
Do you own the *Lemon Aid Lead Alphabet: Where to Find Customers when you run out of Family and Friends?* Have you attended a live Lemon Aid Learning Adventure with the Lemon Aid Lady? Now you can combine the best of both experiences and hear NEW ideas never before taught in a live session or published in the book. This nearly four-hour audio tape set will teach you the A-to-Zs of finding customers in unlikely places with innovative *TWISTS*.
$55.95

Prices and product availability subject to change without notice.

Lemon Aid Learning Adventures. Creating Sweet Successes and Juicy Profits!

Lemon Aid Learning Adventures
P.O. Box 1720
Lake Dallas TX 75065
940-498-0995 www.lemonaidlady.com